Wharfed

The River Wharfe gives its name to one of the loveliest dales of North Yorkshire. From Bolton Abbey upwards to its origins at Cam Beck and Oughtershaw Beck, the road is never more than a few hundred metres from the river; thus visitors can enjoy the sylvan beauty of Wharfedale to the full, although its wild beginnings at Langstrothdale are a little less accessible. The whole dale was once an important hunting chase granted to the Percy fam— and it eventually became t— property of the Dukes of Dev— shire, who replanted and revi— ised the area.

Wharfedale's scenery is dominated by the white scars of limestone rock on the hillsides and each of the villages scattered throughout it has an individual appeal, from the delightfully well-kept village of Burnsall to the busy little tourist centre of Kettlewell, ... a market was established there, but it owes its more recent prosperity to the lead mining which took place nearby in the eighteenth and nineteenth centuries, and more latterly still to the many visitors who exploit its potential as an ideal touring base for the surrounding countryside.

The village of Conistone is built around a small green, and lies tucked beneath the high limestone cliffs of Conistone Pie and Wassa, looking across Wharfedale to Kilnsey Crag. Many of its buildings are of the late seventeenth century and most are built of local limestone, creating a typical dales scene.

On a larger scale is the small town of Grassington, with its delightful cobbled market-place and steep sloping streets beyond. This is another of the main touring

Left: The five-arched bridge at Burnsall
Below: The idyllic scene near Appletreewick

*Left: Shepherding at Conistone
Far left, centre: Appletreewick
Far left, bottom: The River Wharfe at Grassington
Below: Bolton Abbey and the ancient stepping stones across the Wharfe*

centres of Upper Wharfedale, and its importance as such dates from the opening of the Yorkshire Dales Railway from Skipton in 1902, although this was closed to passenger traffic in 1930. The remains of an Iron Age village nearby bear testament to the fact that its popularity as a settlement dates back much earlier than this, however.

Two miles below Burnsall on the east side of Wharfedale is Appletreewick, pronounced locally as 'Aptrick'. This village began to prosper around 1300, when nearby Bolton Priory acquired its manor and associated sheep-farming and lead-mining industries. The main High Street is steep, with High Hall at one end and Low Hall at the other, the Tudor-style High Hall having been restored by Sir William Craven, Appletreewick's own version of Dick Whittington, who became Sheriff and Lord Mayor of London at the beginning of the seventeenth century.

Sadly only the ruins of Bolton Priory itself remain, but these majestic ruins still enjoy an idyllic setting above the curving banks of the River Wharfe, and both Turner and Landseer were inspired by the beauty of the scene to produce memorable paintings. The priory was founded in 1120 and was largely completed by 1220, although there were some later additions. Ironically, the local village is called Bolton Abbey, although the priory with which it is associated has never been an abbey.

Bolton Hall, just to the west of the priory, incorporates the fourteenth-century priory gatehouse.

Littondale

The River Wharfe is joined by the River Skirfare just north-east of Kilnsey Crag, and it is this latter river which flows through the comparatively secluded dale known generally as Littondale, although christened Amerdale by the poet William Wordsworth. Many people who have never visited the dales will be familiar with the scenery of Littondale, for it was originally the setting for the television series *Emmerdale Farm*, although filming now takes place in the Leathley area, near Ilkley.

Littondale is much smaller and quieter than Wharfedale, although the two rivers run roughly parallel and both dales are marked by the towering white limestone cliffs above. The villages of Littondale are generally small and linear, as typified by Halton Gill near the head of the dale. This attractive hamlet is situated 1,000 feet above sea-level on the north side of the river, at the foot of Horse Head Pass, an old packhorse route to Raisgill in Langstrothdale. It has a large proportion of seventeenth-century buildings and an attractive barn with a splendid porch, dated 1829, with the builders' initials proudly carved on it.

Also situated on the north side of the dale is the quiet little village of Hawkswick, with its elegant seventeenth- and eighteenth-century houses. On the south side of the river, further upstream, is the largest of Littondale's settlements — Arncliffe. The main part of the village is dominated by a spacious green overlooked by delightful cottages, but St Oswald's Church, just to the north, is also well worth a visit, with its pleasant porch, stout medieval tower and riverside setting. Inside the church there is a list of the Arncliffe men who fought at Flodden Field in 1531. There are also many splendid riverside walks along this section of the dale.

Below: Autumn in Littondale
Right: Looking towards Littondale and Arncliffe

Left: Arncliffe Church and bridge, Littondale
Below: Beckermonds, Langstrothdale

In spite of, or perhaps because of, its scarcity of settlements, Littondale is one of the most attractive of the Yorkshire Dales. It is scattered with magnificent barns, some of which have now been tastefully converted into private residences. Most of the limestone cottages reflect in the pitch of their roofs the slope of the fells beyond them.

Running roughly parallel to the upper reaches of Littondale is Langstrothdale, the name given to the wilder upper reaches of Wharfedale above Buckden. Langstrothdale Chase was formerly a hunting area for deer and game, although the natural woodland now diminishes beyond Yockenthwaite. Just above Yockenthwaite, hidden behind a wall in a field across the river, is one of the few Bronze Age stone circles in the dales, with twenty stones forming a rough circle about twenty-five feet across.

An impressive network of roads provides good access to Langstrothdale, and at Beckermonds a fork in the road gives the visitor an enviable choice of direction. The northern arm of the road climbs first to Oughtershaw, at 1,200 feet, and then to the watershed on Fleet Moss, at 1,934 feet the highest road in North Yorkshire, before descending to Wensleydale at Hawes. The southern arm from Beckermonds continues westwards to High Greenfield. Greenfield was a grange of Fountains Abbey, so this route probably originated in medieval times.

Nidderdale

Nidderdale is quite different from the other dales because the River Nidd, which flows through it, is now harnessed in three reservoirs – Gouthwaite, Scar House and Angram – which combine to provide water for the city of Bradford. Even before their arrival, however, Nidderdale was the most industrialised of the dales, with flax-growing, the manufacture of linen and hemp, and lead-ore mining all taking place in the vicinity.

At the southern end of Gouthwaite Reservoir is Ramsgill, which is one of Nidderdale's prettiest villages, vying perhaps with Pateley Bridge for the honour of being the most attractive. Pateley Bridge developed as a market centre in the fourteenth century, but it reached the peak of its importance and prosperity in about 1800, when the textile industry began to flourish there too.

Knaresborough, situated where the Nidd finally cuts through a deep gorge of limestone and flows out on to an open plain, was also once an important textile centre. It is dominated by a fourteenth-century castle.

On the road between Pateley Bridge and Brimham lie the Brimham Rocks, an area of gritstone outcrops which extends over fifty acres. Fantastic and sometimes grotesque shapes have been carved in the rocks by wind, water and frost, and many of them have been given bizarre names such as

'The Turtle', 'The Dancing Bear' and 'The Kissing Chair'.

Equally unusual are the Stump Cross Caverns which are between Pateley Bridge and Grassington – an extensive cave system which was once occupied by wild animals and which was discovered by lead-miners in the 1850s. Fantastic stalactites and stalagmites can be seen in the show cave.

Below left: Knaresborough, on the banks of the Nidd
Below: Pastoral peace near Pateley Bridge
Right: Brimham Rocks

Castles & Abbeys

The Yorkshire Dales are richly steeped in history, a history which is embodied in the many magnificent castles and abbeys scattered throughout the area.

Amongst the castles, Richmond, Skipton and Bolton are perhaps the most impressive. Richmond Castle's origins are Norman and its present-day ruins, perched dramatically on steep cliffs above the town, form a magnificent sight. Skipton Castle, which has an equally dramatic setting high above the Eller Beck gorge, is also Norman, having been built by the de Romilles. Bolton Castle, in Wensleydale, is one of the finest examples of a fourteenth-century fortified mansion in England, its most romantic claim to fame being that Mary Queen of Scots was held prisoner there for eight months in 1568.

During the course of history, various monasteries have also extended their influence over the dales and as a result there are many remains of religious buildings. Fountains Abbey was once the most important of them all. Established in the twelfth century, the abbey subsequently grew into one of the richest monastic houses in England because of its vast revenues from wool. The site of Rievaulx Abbey, across the Vale of the York, on the North York Moors, was granted to the Cistercians in 1131, but they also owned land in the dales. Many of the abbeys in the dales were badly desecrated at the time of the Dissolution, nonetheless the ruins which remain today are still magnificent in their own right.

Clockwise from top left: Bolton Castle, Richmond Castle, Skipton Castle, Fountains Abbey, Jervaulx Abbey

Swaledale

Swaledale, the most northerly of the major dales, has an almost austere beauty, its swept landscape often punctuated only by isolated farm buildings made from the local grey-brown sandstone. Upper Swaledale is particularly remote, and above the charming hamlet of Keld – at 1,100 feet above sea-level, one of England's most isolated villages – it could almost be described as a wilderness, although the early Norsemen who settled and brought their native type of farming here flourished precisely because the rugged and steep fells so closely resembled their own countryside. The warm, durable wool produced by the Swaledale sheep is also a direct result of the somewhat harsh environment.

The delightful village of Muker is separated from Keld by the great mass of Kisdon Hill, a superb vantage-point for breathtaking views over Swaledale. Kisdon Force, near Keld, is a dramatic fall on the River Swale between

Left: Flower-filled meadows in Upper Swaledale
Left, inset: The hump-backed bridge at Thwaite
Below: The tumbling waters of Kisdon Force

two great walls of limestone, whilst East Gill Force is another waterfall on a small tributary of the Swale.

Thwaite is another typical dales village, with a little hump-backed bridge across the river and many houses built from the local grey stone. It is famous as the birthplace of Richard and Cherry Kearton, who were educated at Muker school and who became world-famous as naturalists and wildlife photographers. They are commemorated by small tablets on either side of the school door at Muker. It is little wonder that the Keartons were inspired with a love of nature, for the stretch between Thwaite and Keld is arguably the most beautiful part of the 270-mile Pennine Way.

South of Thwaite is the Buttertubs Pass, named after the series of potholes on both sides of the road to Hawes. Their name is derived either from their resemblance to the old-fashioned butter tubs or from the memory of farmers on their way to market, lowering their butter into the holes to cool off while they rested. The Pass rises to a height of 1,726 feet, a little lower than Tan Hill, at 1,732 feet above sea-level, the site of England's highest inn. This lonely outstation is otherwise wild and empty — the inn is the only human habitation in the area

and there is no public transport to it.

Near the pleasant villages of Reeth and Grinton, Swaledale is joined by Arkengarthdale, a dale in which the signs of former lead mining are still very evident and where scattered hamlets and villages are the only settlements. Langthwaite is just one such village, along with the delightfully-named hamlets of Whaw, Booze and Arkle Town, not far away.

At the lower reaches of Swaledale, however, the countryside becomes softer and comparatively more populated, culminating in the bustling market-town of Richmond, which is dominated by the remains of its hilltop Norman castle. Richmond is often described as the northern gateway to the dales, and the castle certainly provides an impressive entrance. Steep cliffs down to the River Swale give the castle an excellent natural defence, as well as providing superb views over the Vale of Mowbray to the east. Strong walls and a massive stone keep protect the town side, whilst at the south-east corner, the eleventh-century Scolland's Hall is probably the oldest hall in England.

The centre of the town itself is dominated by the cobbled market-place, where the Church of Holy Trinity, dating from the early twelfth century, stands. It has now been adapted as a fine museum for the Green Howard Regiment and houses a magnificent collection of miltary memorabilia. Narrow streets radiate from the market-place, giving the town a wonderful atmosphere of the Middle Ages. The present parish church of St Mary in Frenchgate rises from the hillside in a beautiful setting and its chancel has sixteenth-century stalls from nearby Easby Abbey, as well as a remarkable monument to Sir Timothy Hutton which shows him with his wife and twelve children kneeling behind. In the churchyard is the Plague Stone, a sad memorial to more than 1,000 people who died of the plague. Richmond is an ideal base for exploring the wonders of Swaledale, offering good facilities which are within easy reach of the more remote parts of the dale. A trip out to the Wain Wath Falls above Keld, for example, would provide an impressive contrast to the town, as the River Swale tumbles over the rocks of the river bed amid the wooded slopes of Upper Swaledale, reinforcing the impression that Swaledale is an area of unrivalled diversity.

Above: The isolated Tan Hill Inn
Top right: The bustling town of Richmond
Right, insert: Langthwaite, Arkengarthdale
Bottom right: Wain Wath Falls

Wensleydale

Wensleydale is a broader and gentler dale than Swaledale, with numerous individual villages largely devoted to dairy and sheep farming. It is fed by two main valleys – Bishopdale and Coverdale – themselves elongated, richly agricultural dales with many scattered farmsteads. Cotterdale is another adjacent dale forming a sheltered place which is not often visited by invading tourists.

Near the head of Wensleydale is Hawes, at some 700 feet above sea-level the highest market-town in Yorkshire and an ideal centre for touring the upper dale. The old station buildings have been converted into the National Park Information Centre, with the old warehouse converted into the Upper Dales Folk Museum, housing a remarkable collection of dales farming and domestic equipment. Hawes Auction Mart is one of the most important livestock markets in the district, and the other important industry is the manufacture of the famous Wensleydale cheese. Indeed the first Wensleydale cheese factory was opened in Hawes in 1897 by Edward Chapman, a local corn and provision merchant, although it was the monks of Jervaulx Abbey who first introduced to Wensleydale the method of producing the cheese.

Hardraw Force, to the north of

Hawes, is a dramatic ninety-nine-foot-high waterfall set in a natural amphitheatre behind the Green Dragon Inn. Indeed, access to the falls is obtained through the inn itself. The natural acoustics of Hardraw have made it a favourite venue for band contests, the triumphant notes of the instruments only being matched by the tumultuous sounds of the

Far left, top: Hawes
Far left, bottom: Bainbridge
Below: Aysgarth Falls
Right: Regency Folly, near Masham

shimmering curtain of water.

Further west along Wensleydale is Bainbridge, a town with a long-documented history. The Romans established a fort at Bainbridge as far back as AD 80. Today grey stone houses stand on the edge of a lovely green, where the existence of a set of stocks demonstrates that life here has not always been as peaceful as it is today! The custom of horn-blowing between 27 September and Shrovetide only occasionally takes place today, but when it does, it is a reminder that Bainbridge was once on the edge of a huge hunting forest. The River Bain drains from nearby Semerwater – one of only four lakes in Yorkshire – and enters Bainbridge over a fine cascade of waterfalls.

Nearby Askrigg, on the north side of Wensleydale, used to be the main market centre of Upper Wensleydale, but it has now been superseded in this respect by Hawes. It is totally different to sprawling Bainbridge, being very compact with a small cobbled square.

One of the most magnificent sights in Wensleydale, however, is Aysgarth Falls, a breathtaking system of three beautiful falls on the River Ure which descend over a mile between richly wooded banks, forming a fitting climax to a visit to glorious Wensleydale.

Further downstream still, however, is the surprisingly unobtrusive village which gives the dale its name – Wensley. This quiet place obtained its market charter back in the fourteenth century and from the main street there is the entrance to Bolton Hall with its lovely parkland. The village's importance has been overshadowed by that of the neighbouring town of Leyburn, with its prosperous Late Georgian houses and good facilities for exploring the lower reaches of Wensleydale.

Left: The cascading waters of Hardraw Force
Above: Fishing on the River Ure

Natural History

Reg Jones

The rivers of the dales, especially in their upper reaches, are fast-flowing. The water is pure and well-aerated, supporting an appreciable amount of life, including the aquatic larval stages of many insects, such as mayflies, on which fish, notably brown trout, feed. This submerged life is largely unseen, but the many river birds are more easily observed. The dipper flies fast and low, up and downstream, uttering a metallic 'clink' as it goes. In contrast, the grey wagtail moves in leisurely bounding flight above the water, taking insects on the wing, settling on wet pebbles to snatch grubs and tiny snails.

Riverbanks are brightened by a succession of flowers: common plants such as marsh marigolds in spring, spotted orchids and meadowsweet in summer. Others which are less familiar, like the grass of Parnassus, also occur. These are all natives, but one foreign species, the golden-flowered mimulus, provides a vivid splash of colour by many banksides in July and August.

Away from the water, there is much to interest the naturalist: there are lime-rich areas, notably in Upper Wharfedale, Ribblesdale and Malhamdale, and lime-free country more in evidence in the north and east of the region.

Kilnsey Crag and Malham Cove are impressive limestone cliffs and between the two is an upland area showing many of the features of limestone country. At various points where limestone pavements are exposed, the deep crevices, or 'grikes', harbour shade-loving plants such as hart's-tongue fern and herb Robert. On the associated limestone pastures, yellow rock-roses and mountain pansies bloom, with bird's-eye primroses in damper situations. In rocky gullies, mosses and ferns like the common polypody flourish, together with rare plants such as the mountain avens. It is to such places that wheatears and ring ouzels come to nest in spring. In side-valleys such as Littondale, the steep slopes are marked by scars and screes with ash trees, which prefer calcareous soils,

Clockwise from top right: Dipper, herb Robert, polypody, bloody cranesbill, wheatear, Mayfly, hart's tongue fern

often maintaining a precarious hold. More complete woodland is found in the valley bottoms. In this area, Grass Wood and Bastow Wood beside the Wharfe at Conistone have ash together with wych elm. There is a rich ground flora which includes herb Paris, bloody cranesbill and several orchids. Such woods also hold a good selection of birds.

Similar features can be seen around Ingleborough: a superb limestone pavement at Scar Close and a fine ash wood at Colt Park.

On high ground where the underlying rock is deficient in lime and the climate is cold and wet, acid peat accumulates and there is moorland vegetation. In less exposed parts, heather or ling is the dominant plant. The tender shoots of heather are the food of red grouse, and grouse moors, seen at their best in Lower Wharfedale and Swaledale, are carefully tended.

On the bleaker 'tops' there are grass moors with considerable stretches of cotton grass, the silken tufted heads of which often brighten an otherwise desolate scene in summer. In very wet parts where the ground is waterlogged are tremulous blankets of sphagnum moss with tufts of rushes, sundews and bog asphodels.

In these uplands are many moorland birds. Skylarks and meadow pipits are abundant, and several waders are summer residents. The bubbling call of a curlew is a typical dales sound. Golden plovers and dunlins also breed. Of the birds of prey, the kestrel is the most common, with casual sightings of others such as the buzzard, merlin and short-eared owl.

Ribblesdale

The river which gives its name to Ribblesdale, one of the southern dales, begins at Ribblehead in the Pennines and follows a winding course southwards towards Settle. It is overlooked by the majestic profiles of Yorkshire's famous three peaks – Ingleborough, Whernside and Pen-y-Ghent, three great blocks of limestone topped by millstone grit – which make this area classic potholing country. Alum Pot and Hull Pot are just two of the best-known potholes in the area, but other less natural gashes in the countryside also exist, caused by the extensive limestone and slate quarrying which continues to take place.

Horton-in-Ribblesdale near the head of the dale is only a small village, but it has been in existence at least since Domesday. It is a good touring centre, with many charming buildings which have made good use of the surrounding slate beds in their construction.

Westwards from Horton is the peak of Ingleborough (2,373 feet) which has some delightful waterfalls, such as Thornton Force, cascading at intervals down its sides. Also skirting the southern flanks of Ingleborough is the delightfully-wooded village of Clapham, which straddles Clapham Beck, whose little ravine is crossed by no fewer than four bridges. Although quite small, Clapham has produced some famous progeny: the village blacksmith was James Faraday, father of Michael Faraday the pioneer of electrical science; Reginald Farrer, the founder of English rock gardening, who travelled the world collecting plants to bring many new species back to England, was

Above: The rolling hills of Ribblesdale
Top right: St Akelda Church, Giggleswick
Centre right: The River Ribble near Settle
Bottom right: Thornton Force and Ingleborough Fell

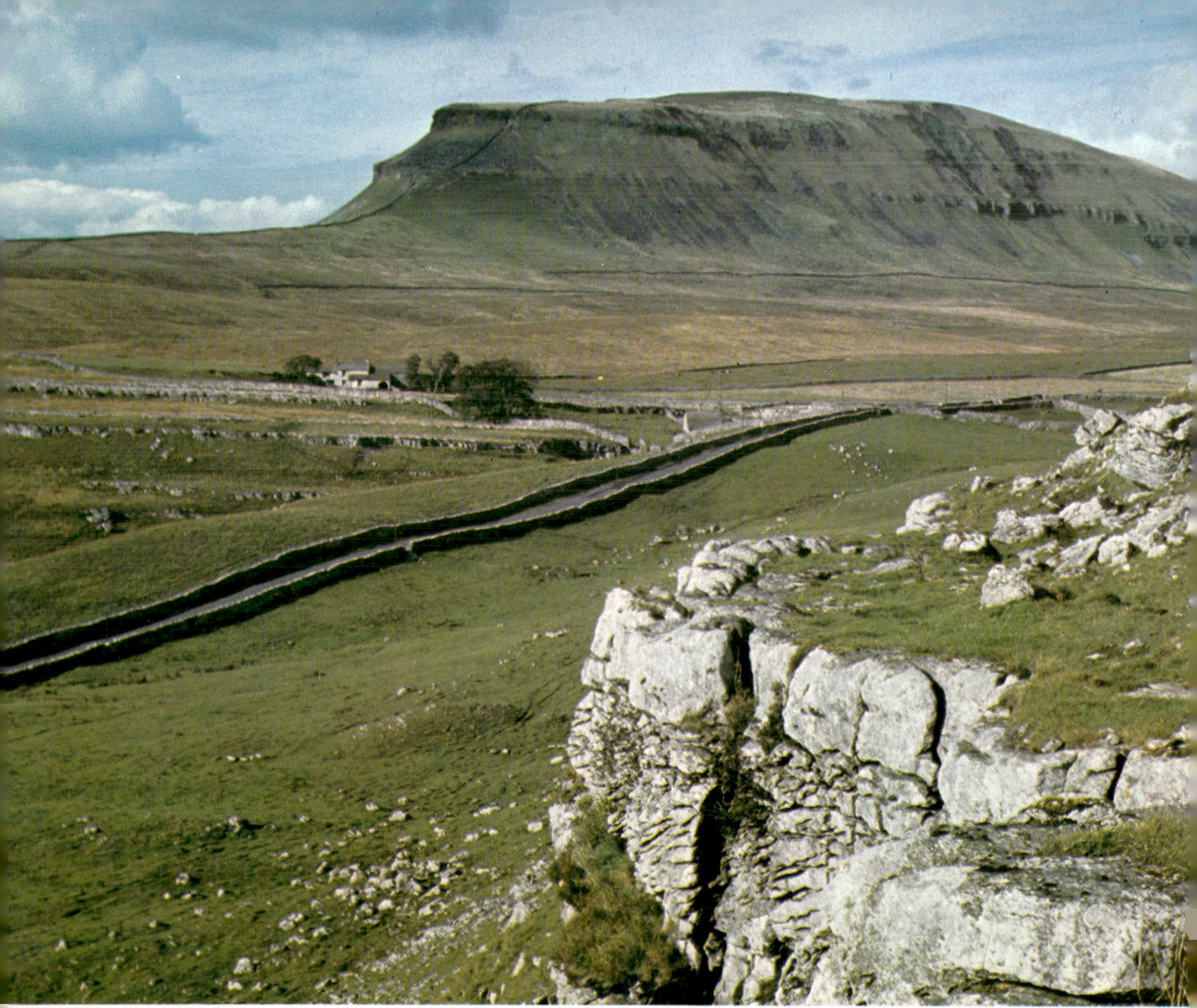

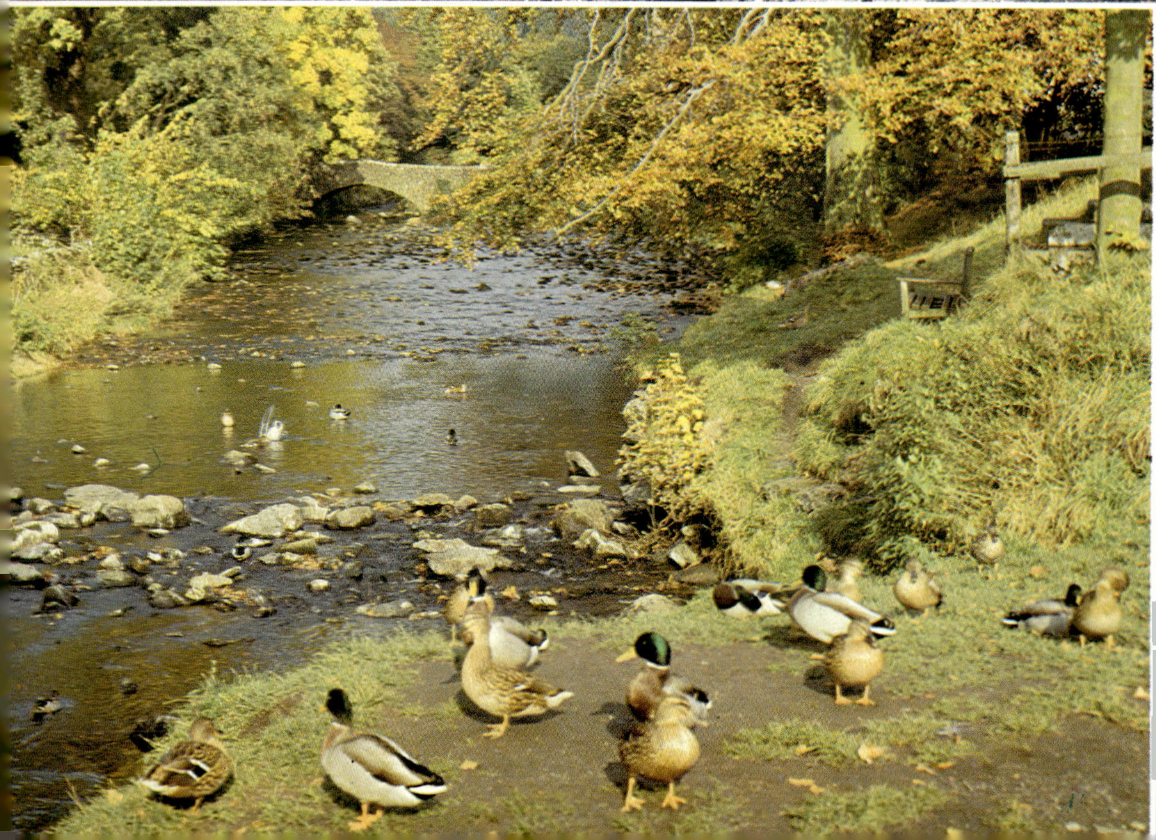

born here; and in 1939 the *Yorkshire Dalesman*, or the *Dalesman* as it is now known — one of the most successful regional magazines in Britain — was founded in Clapham.

The famous Ingleborough Cave is only a mile and a half from Clapham, and the cave itself is about a mile in length, all of which is well endowed with stalactites, stalagmites and fairy-tale pools. Nearby Gaping Gill is one of the most dramatic potholes in the country, with a main chamber large enough to accommodate York Minster, whilst White Scar Cave is yet another natural underground drainage system of Ingleborough, complete with waterfalls and other remarkable formations which are now spectacularly flood-lit for the public.

To return to the River Ribble itself, however, below Horton it passes through Stainforth, with its charmingly-shaped seventeenth-century packhorse bridge, and just below the village is Stainforth Force, where the river cascades over several limestone ledges into a deep, broad pool. From there it proceeds almost due south towards Giggleswick and Settle, not actually passing through the latter settlement but curving instead into Giggleswick. Settle's market charter goes as far back as 1249 and there is still a definite aura of times gone by, with small, independent shops surrounding its compact market-place.

In medieval times the village of Giggleswick was part of the extensive Percy properties. Now it is home to a well-known public school, the great copper dome of whose chapel is an outstanding landmark, as well as a charming church dedicated to St Akelda. This church actually dates from the twelfth century, although most of the existing building dates from the fifteenth century. It has a long, low profile with no interior division between the nave and chancel. Nearby are several fine seventeenth-century buildings made from pale local limestone.

Left: Pen-y-Ghent and the limestone cliffs near Settle
Below left: Riverbank scene near Clapham
Below: Stainforth Force, Upper Ribblesdale

Malhamdale

Malhamdale is the name given to the upper valley of the River Aire, and at its beginnings it has the dramatic scenery of all limestone country — rocky cliffs, steep gorges and tumbling streams. But Malhamdale's geology also sets it apart from the other dales to a certain extent, for it is traversed by geological faults which have left great cliffs, such as Giggleswick Scar on the road between Ingleton and Settle. Gordale Scar is also found in Malhamdale, a gigantic collapsed cave system situated about one and a half miles east of Malham, where a moorland stream has cut its way through the limestone cliff to form a vast gorge. Towering masses of rock overlook the gorge, some of them overhanging, and nearby there is a delightful little waterfall known as Janet's Foss, reputedly named after the queen of the local fairies.

The nearest village to Gordale

Scar is Malham, formerly a famous centre for livestock markets, but now Malhamdale's most visited village. It is an attractive place, with an old bridge crossing the rushing waters of the

Below left: The approach to Gordale Scar, near Malham
Below: Malham Cove
Right: The Leeds and Liverpool Canal passes through the heart of Skipton

River Aire, and makes a good base for visiting Malham Tarn and Malham Cove. The tarn is a 153-acre glacial lake that owes its existence to the uplifting of strata by the North Craven Fault. It is overlooked by Malham Tarn House, built by the millionaire Walter Morrison, but now used as a field studies centre. It is said that Charles Kingsley, a former visitor to the house, was inspired by its surroundings to write *The Water Babies*.

Nearby Malham Cove is a splendid 300-foot-high semicircle of overhanging limestone rock with fascinating limestone pavements above it.

Further downstream from Malham is the small village of Kirkby Malham, set in a wooded valley which runs westwards from the Aire. It has a fine seventeenth-century vicarage and a Perpendicular church which inside has the sad brass memorial to a brother and sister who died the same day in 1673, aged only six and twelve. One of Oliver Cromwell's most trusted officers, General John Lambert, once lived at nearby Calton Hall.

Forming a stark contrast to the dramatic sights of the upper dale is the bustling town of Skipton, situated in the Aire Gap. Known as 'the southern gateway to the dales', Skipton is a thriving centre of communications and a busy market centre in its own right. It was originally settled by Anglian sheepfarmers in the seventh century, becoming a Norman stronghold in the twelfth century when Skipton Castle was built. The parish church grew up at the same time as the castle and the town developed down the High Street. Many of the existing High Street properties were rebuilt in the seventeenth century.

Left: Malham Tarn
Above: The steep sides of Gordale Scar

Geology

The unique landscape of the Yorkshire Dales has largely been created by the huge limestone deposits which are found there, deposits which have been shifted by massive earth movements and scoured by glacial action, creating what is known as a 'karst landscape'.

Limestone is actually created by the build-up of the shells of millions of sea animals over many thousands of years, and more than 330 million years ago the area covered by the Yorkshire Dales was, in fact, a shallow tropical sea. Later, massive earth movements folded and fractured the rocks, causing enormous faults and cracks which also provided pathways for hot fluids carrying lead and other mineral deposits. Next, the landscape was carved by the erosive powers of glaciers and subsequent meltwater during and after the Ice Age, creating such features as the broad floors and steep sides of the dales, as well as the crags, pavements and caves.

The powerful combination of glaciers and water with limestone is nowhere better demonstrated than in the limestone pavements which can be found in places like Malham Cove. Here glaciers have scoured the limestone, whilst rainwater has slowly eaten into the fractures of the rock, opening them into 'grikes' and leaving solid blocks, or 'clints' in between. Eventually some of the

Below left: The Buttertubs
Below right: Glacial boulder
Bottom: Limestone pavement, Malham Cove
Right: Rock pillar, Pen-y-Ghent

gulleys open up into underground streams, as the rainwater continues to dissolve the limestone, producing a chemical solution which percolates deeper and deeper into the substrata.

Sometimes huge underground caves are formed by the percolating water, often linked together by a series of underground streams and rivers. The surface topography remains dry in many cases, giving the impression that some of the dales are dry valleys.

There are also literally thousands of potholes in the Yorkshire Dales, from small fissures to massive rifts such as Alum Pot, which has a spectacular spray-blown entrance. Sometimes there are whole series of potholes situated together, such as at the Buttertubs, which are about twenty metres deep and which cut into almost the whole depth of the limestone at that point.

But not all the geological oddities are underground. Scattered across the surface of the dales are huge limestone crags which have been sculptured by glaciers, wind and rain. Kilnsey Crag, for example, towers 170 feet above the surrounding landscape, and has a dramatic recessed base where a former glacier has scoured it.

These then are just some of the more dramatic geological features to be found in the Yorkshire Dales, features which combine with the gentler pastoral scene to produce an area whose beauty and fascination is unrivalled.

Top: Hunt Pot
Above left: Kilnsey Crag
Above right: Gordale Scar